Defining
MOMENTS
OVERCOMING CHALLENGES

Jean
DRISCOLL

Dream Big, Work Hard!

by Michael Sandler

CONSULTANT
Jean Driscoll

BEARPORT
PUBLISHING

New York, New York

Credits

Cover and title page, © AP/Wide World Photos; 4, Courtesy of the Driscoll family; 5, © Darren McCollester/Getty Images; 6, Courtesy of the Driscoll family; 7, Courtesy of the Driscoll family; 8, Courtesy of the Driscoll family; 9, Courtesy of the Driscoll family; 10, Courtesy of the Driscoll family; 11, Courtesy of the Driscoll family; 12, Courtesy of the Driscoll family; 13, Courtesy of the Driscoll family; 14, Courtesy of Cindy Owens Housner; 15, Courtesy of the Driscoll family; 16, Courtesy of the Driscoll family; 17, © Curt Beamer; 18, © Curt Beamer; 19, Courtesy of the Driscoll family; 20, Courtesy of the Driscoll family; 21, Courtesy of the Driscoll family; 22, Courtesy of the Driscoll family; 23, Courtesy of the Driscoll family; 24, © Fay Foto/Boston Athletic Association; 25, © Timothy A. Clary/AFP/Getty Images; 26, © Victor Sailer /Boston Athletic Association; 27, Courtesy of the Driscoll family.

Publisher: Kenn Goin
Project Editor: Lisa Wiseman
Creative Director: Spencer Brinker
Original Design: Fabia Wargin

Library of Congress Cataloging-in-Publication Data

Sandler, Michael.
    Jean Driscoll : dream big, work hard! / by Michael Sandler.
        p. cm. — (Defining moments. Overcoming challenges)
    Includes bibliographical references and index.
    ISBN-13: 978-1-59716-268-5 (library binding)
    ISBN-10: 1-59716-268-X (library binding)
    ISBN-13: 978-1-59716-296-8 (pbk.)
    ISBN-10: 1-59716-296-5 (pbk.)
    1. Driscoll, Jean, 1966– 2. Athletes—United States—Biography—Juvenile literature. 3. People with disabilities—United States—Biography—Juvenile literature. 4. Spina bifida—Patients—United States—Biography—Juvenile literature. 5. Wheelchair sports—United States—Juvenile literature. I. Title. II. Series.

    GV697.D75S26 2007
    796.092—dc22

                                    2006005827

For more information, write to Bearport Publishing Company, Inc.,
101 Fifth Avenue, Suite 6R, New York, New York 10003.
Printed in the United States of America.

1 2 3 4 5 6 7 8 9 10

Table of Contents

Now or Never

Jean knew this was her chance. She needed to take the lead in order to win the 2000 Boston **Marathon**. With a victory, she'd become the only athlete ever to win the race eight times.

Three times before she had tried. Three times before she had failed. Jean was **determined** that this race was going to be different.

Louise Sauvage (left) and Jean Driscoll (right) as they wait for the start of the 2000 Boston Marathon

About 20,000 people take part in the Boston Marathon each year.

Jean had reached Heartbreak Hill, the toughest part of the marathon. Louise Sauvage, her **rival**, was right at her side. Winning wasn't going to be easy.

The brutal climb began. Every muscle in Jean's body screamed for her to stop. Her mind fought against her body. *Work harder!*

Growing Up the Hard Way

Jean Driscoll knew about working hard. She was born with spina bifida, a condition that affects the **spinal cord** and the **vertebrae**.

Since childhood, everything was harder for Jean, especially walking. To stay balanced, she had to turn her feet and ankles outward.

Spina bifida occurs when the spine doesn't form properly. A baby born with spina bifida has an opening in the spine. Most often this opening is in the middle or lower part of the back. This **birth defect** can lead to **disabilities**.

Jean (left) wearing leg braces at age four. Next to Jean are her twin brothers, Ray and Ron, as well as her sister, Francie (right).

Jean fell down often, however, despite wearing steel braces. The braces looked ugly. The metal parts squeaked loudly. Other kids teased her.

Still, the braces let her move around by herself. For longer distances, she was pulled in a wagon by her sister and her brothers.

Jean longed to be free. She wished she could run and play without having to work at it.

Not letting her leg braces stop her,
Jean dances at a family wedding.

Freedom and Loss

When Jean was nine years old, she taught herself how to ride a bike. Finally, she had freedom. She could get around by herself, moving like the wind!

Then just before her 14th birthday, Jean had a terrible accident. She turned too sharply around a corner and fell to the ground.

As a child, Jean used to stare at her sister's sports trophies with envy. Despite her physical disability, Jean dreamed of being an athlete.

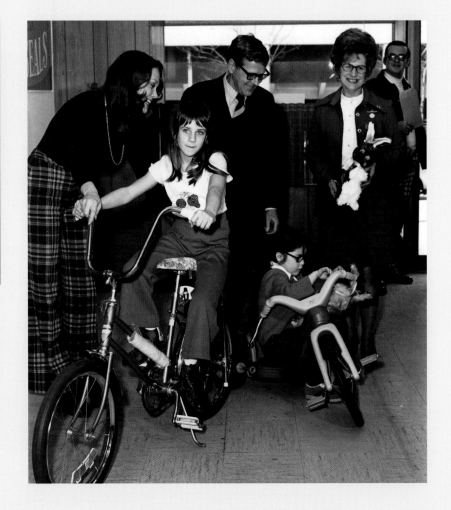

Jean (left) on a bike at age ten

Jean (left) and a friend celebrate their eighth grade graduation.

In the hospital, Jean learned that her hip was badly damaged. She would need several operations.

Worst of all, she would need to wear a body cast for months. Jean could forget about riding her bike. She wouldn't be able to go to school. Jean wouldn't even be able to move. Her freedom was gone.

It's Not Fair

The cast was a prison for Jean. She dreamed of escaping from it. She wanted to ride her bike. She wanted to walk, maybe even better than before.

When the cast came off, however, there was more bad news. The operations had failed. Jean would need crutches and a wheelchair for the rest of her life.

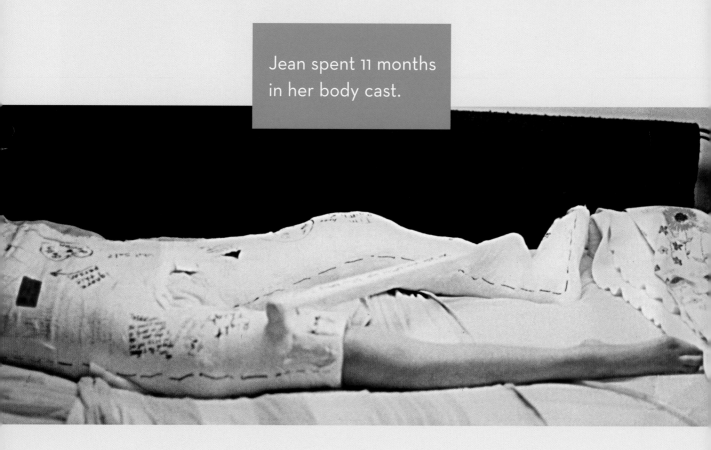

Jean spent 11 months in her body cast.

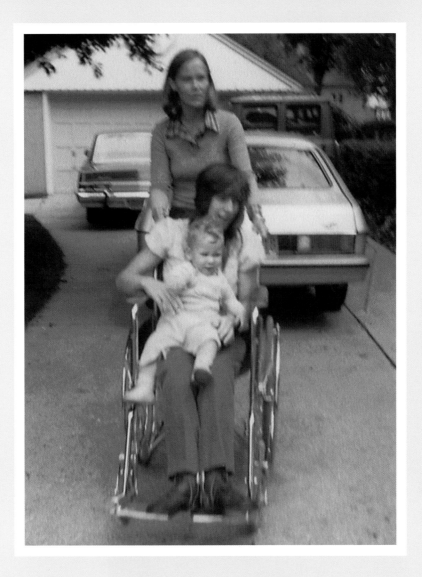

Jean's first wheelchair

Jean was **devastated**. Other kids led normal lives. Her sister, Francie, went on dates, went to dances, and had a job. Why couldn't she?

Jean stared at her crutches and wheelchair. *I hate them*, she thought. She refused to use them. Then she suddenly changed her mind.

Starting Over

Jean realized that to move around by herself she would need the crutches and the wheelchair. It would be a struggle to get used to them. However, Jean was determined to make it work.

The next fall, Jean entered a new high school. There, she met other students in wheelchairs.

Jean wore braces and used crutches to help her walk in high school. Here she is with her friend Kathie Martin.

One of Jean's friends, Jim Ratzburg, kept pestering her. He wanted her to try wheelchair soccer.

At first, Jean refused. "Come on," she told Jim. "You can't play soccer without good legs."

Jim, however, wouldn't take no for an answer. Finally, Jean gave in and **accompanied** him to a practice. What Jean discovered changed her life.

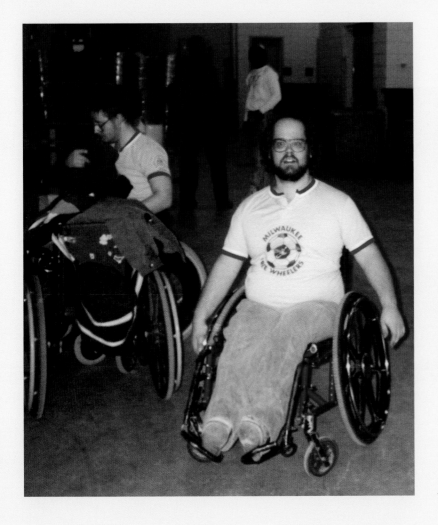

Jim Ratzburg

In wheelchair soccer, players don't kick the ball. Instead, they throw the ball to one another and toward the goal.

Fast and Wild

Wheelchair soccer was nothing like Jean expected. It was fast. It was wild. It was the coolest thing she had ever done!

"Chairs were crashing and banging; bodies were flying," she remembers.

Over the next few months, she tried one wheelchair sport after another: racing, tennis, ice hockey, and even waterskiing. Jean was hooked.

Jean holding a trophy that she won following a national wheelchair soccer tournament

Jean loves to water-ski.

There was only one problem. Jean played so hard that she often wrecked her wheelchair. Her family couldn't afford to fix it.

Luckily, the sports group Jean played for agreed to pay for repairs. Jean was too good for them to risk losing her.

After high school, Jean went to the University of Illinois. She earned two degrees there, a bachelor of arts and a master's.

College Athlete

When Jean went to the University of Illinois, she kept playing wheelchair sports. She concentrated on basketball and racing. She didn't have time for anything else.

Jean would spend endless hours in the gym building her strength and **stamina**. She did long training rides on country roads. She also practiced with the basketball team each day.

Jean climbs a rope during a workout

Jean on the basketball court

Each night, Jean just wanted to fall right into bed. First, however, she had to finish her homework.

Still, the practice and training paid off. Her basketball team was unstoppable and her race results were just as impressive. She won one event after another.

New Goals

Jean was becoming a star college athlete. She was even earning victories in **international** contests like the 1988 Paralympic Games. There, Jean won four medals, including a gold in the 4 × 200-meter **relay**.

Jean's coach, Marty Morse, was encouraged by her success. He wanted her to try longer distance races. He wanted her to compete in the longest race of all—the marathon!

The Paralympic Games are the Olympics for people with physical disabilities. They are held the same year and in the same place as the Olympics.

Jean (left) racing during the 1996 Paralympics

18

Jean training with coach Marty Morse

Jean **protested** at first. "I don't want to do a marathon!" she said. "It's way too long."

Marty kept trying to convince her. He saw her talent and determination. He believed she could be the best. Finally, Jean agreed to give it a try.

The Marathon

As Marty suspected, Jean was made for the marathon. She came in second in her very first race. Only University of Illinois teammate Ann Cody finished faster.

After the race, Jean's coach ran up to her. "You **qualified** for the Boston Marathon!" he exclaimed.

Marty created special exercises to help Jean and Ann train. He had them take turns towing other wheelchair athletes. Jean sometimes pulled 700 pounds (318 kg) across a parking lot.

Teammate Ann Cody with Jean

Jean training for the marathon

Jean couldn't believe it! The Boston Marathon was the most famous race in the world—and the toughest. It was known for its steep hills. The worst ones came at the end, just when racers were the most tired.

To prepare, Jean trained harder than ever. She practiced with Ann. They worked together **relentlessly**.

Boston

On April 16, 1990, race day finally arrived. The marathon began. By mile eight, Jean was at the front of the pack. Alongside her were Ann and a few other racers.

Jean kept punching the **pushrim** on her wheels. She reached the brutal hills. Up and down she went. By mile 20, only Ann was still with her. Jean stroked the wheels harder.

Then she turned her head. No one was there! She had the lead all to herself. Jean pumped and pumped, refusing to let up until she glided across the finish line. Jean hadn't just won the race, she'd done it faster than anyone else in history.

Jean celebrates her win

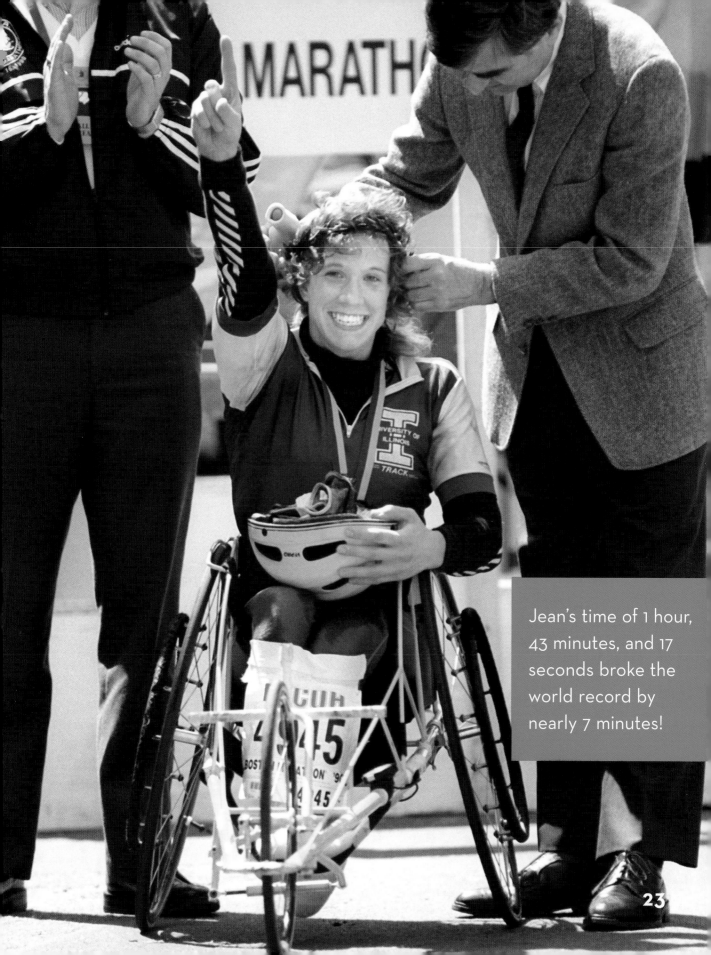

Jean's time of 1 hour, 43 minutes, and 17 seconds broke the world record by nearly 7 minutes!

Queen of the Race

The 1990 marathon was just the beginning. Jean kept returning to Boston and setting new records. She won it again, and again, and again. She took first place seven years in a row! Jean was queen of the marathon.

Then, in 1997, Jean crashed her wheelchair and lost the race. The following two years, Jean narrowly lost to rival Louise Sauvage.

Jean after winning the 1992 Boston Marathon

Louise Sauvage narrowly beats Jean to the finish line during the 1998 Boston Marathon

Jean's second-place finishes were heartbreakingly close. She lost by less than a second in both 1998 and 1999.

Briefly, Jean thought about giving up. Maybe she wasn't meant to win the race eight times. Then she thought about how far she'd come. She couldn't quit now. For the 2000 marathon, she decided to train even harder!

Eight Victories

Midway through the 2000 marathon, Jean found herself tied for the lead. Louise was right by her side. Twice, Jean broke away. Twice, Louise caught up.

The third time was different. On Heartbreak Hill, Jean pulled away for good.

The crowd roared as Jean snapped the finish line tape. She had done it. Somehow a little girl with leg braces had grown up to win the Boston Marathon—eight times!

Jean isn't just the only eight-time winner of the Boston Marathon. She is also the only person to break the world record five different times.

Achieving her dream, Jean wins her eighth Boston Marathon.

Jean travels around the country speaking to adults and children. She shares the story of how she overcame challenges in her life.

Today, Jean talks to people about setting goals that seem impossible. "Dream big and work hard," she says, noting her own experience.

Once, she had feared that a wheelchair would limit her life. Instead, it allowed many wonderful dreams to come true.

Just the Facts

■ Jean is also an Olympic athlete. She won the silver medal at both the 1992 and 1996 Olympics in the 800 meter wheelchair event. She went on to win the gold medal at the 2000 Paralympics in Sydney, Australia.

■ Today, Jean's 1994 time (1:34:22) is still the course record for the women's wheelchair division at the Boston Marathon. No one has even come close to breaking it!

Timeline

Here are some important events in Jean Driscoll's life.

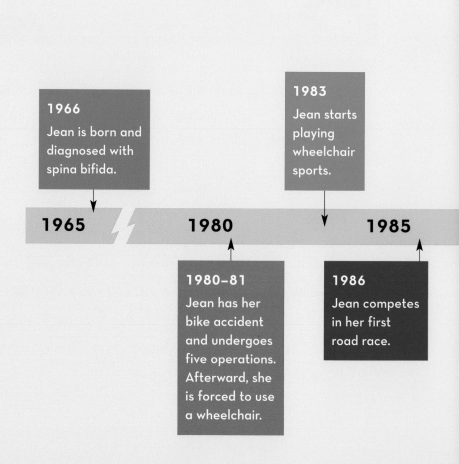

1966
Jean is born and diagnosed with spina bifida.

1983
Jean starts playing wheelchair sports.

1965   **1980**   **1985**

1980–81
Jean has her bike accident and undergoes five operations. Afterward, she is forced to use a wheelchair.

1986
Jean competes in her first road race.

■ To celebrate her extraordinary career as a top wheelchair racer, the Royal Caribbean cruise line named Jean godmother of the ship *Mariner of the Seas*. This is the highest honor in the cruise ship industry.

■ Spina bifida affects people in different ways. Some people are left **paralyzed**. Others need lots of medical care throughout their lives. Jean has a lump on her back and nerve damage that affects her legs.

■ Today, doctors know that when women take folic acid, a vitamin, before and during pregnancy, it can help prevent spina bifida in their children.

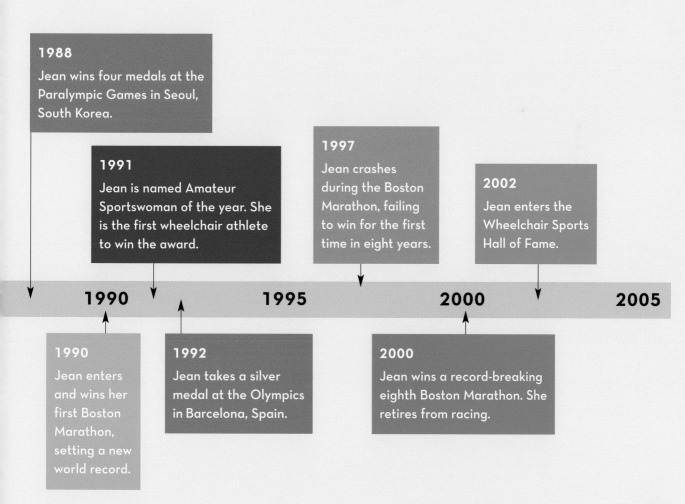

1988
Jean wins four medals at the Paralympic Games in Seoul, South Korea.

1991
Jean is named Amateur Sportswoman of the year. She is the first wheelchair athlete to win the award.

1997
Jean crashes during the Boston Marathon, failing to win for the first time in eight years.

2002
Jean enters the Wheelchair Sports Hall of Fame.

1990

1995

2000

2005

1990
Jean enters and wins her first Boston Marathon, setting a new world record.

1992
Jean takes a silver medal at the Olympics in Barcelona, Spain.

2000
Jean wins a record-breaking eighth Boston Marathon. She retires from racing.

Glossary

accompanied (uh-KUM-puh-need) went somewhere with someone

birth defect (BURTH DEE-fekt) a condition that is present when a baby is born

determined (di-TUR-mind) having made up one's mind to do something

devastated (DEV-uh-*stay*-tid) terribly shocked or upset

disabilities (*diss*-uh-BIL-uh-teez) conditions that make it hard for people to go about their daily activities

international (*in*-ter-NASH-uh-nuhl) involving people from countries around the world

marathon (MAR-uh-thon) a foot or wheelchair race that covers 26.2 miles (42.2 km)

paralyzed (PA-ruh-lyezd) unable to move parts of one's body

protested (PROH-test-id) tried to say no; objected

pushrim (PUSH-rim) the circular metal piece attached to a wheel that is used to make a wheelchair move; the area where a person grabs the wheel to push

qualified (KWAHL-uh-fyed) earned a place in

relay (REE-lay) a team event in which members take turns racing for their team

relentlessly (ri-LENT-less-lee) in a very determined way, without stopping or getting tired

rival (RYE-vuhl) someone who is competing against another person

spinal cord (SPY-nuhl KORD) nerve tissue that runs down a person's back and carries messages from the brain to nerves in the body

stamina (STAM-uh-nuh) strength and energy used to do something for a long period of time

vertebrae (VUR-tuh-*bray*) the bones that form the backbone

Bibliography

Driscoll, Jean, and Janet and Geoff Benge. *Determined to Win.* Colorado Springs, CO: Shaw Books (2001).

sportsillustrated.cnn.com/athletics/
2000/boston_marathon/news/2000/
04/17/marathon_wheelchair_ap/

www.jeandriscoll.com

www.sbaa.org

Read More

Kent, Deborah. *Athletes With Disabilities.* New York: Franklin Watts (2003).

Kulper, Eileen. *The Boston Marathon.* Mankato, MN: Creative Education (1992).

Little, James R. *Wheelchair Road Racing.* Mankato, MN: Capstone Press (1998).

Oxlade, Chris, and David Ballheimer. *Olympics.* New York: DK Publishing (2000).

Learn More Online

Visit these Web sites to learn more about Jean Driscoll, wheelchair sports, and the Boston Marathon:

www.boston.com/marathon/history/womens_wheelchair_champions.htm
www.usolympicteam.com/paralympics/
www.will.uiuc.edu/tv/documentaries/atw/atw.html

Index

About the Author

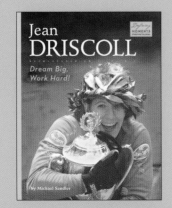

MICHAEL SANDLER lives and writes in Brooklyn, New York. He has written numerous books on sports for children and young adults.